babette

DESIGNING A VISION

ISBN 978-1-60585-226-3

Introduction

Throughout my career, I've always been excited about the future:

the next idea, the next fabric, the next collection. New challenges feed my creative soul.

Taking a backward look, as I've done in this portfolio of images from my four decades of design work, has also been inspiring and enriching. As I sifted through these beautiful photographs, I saw how my designs have evolved over the decades in response to women's changing roles in society. In the 1980s, shoulder pads made a statement about women's empowerment. Now we express our power less overtly. I've also been strongly influenced by changing developments in fabric technology. More than twenty years ago, I was one of the first American designers to embrace the potential of polyester microfiber. Today I'm excited by new memory fabrics that can look as rumpled or smooth as the wearer wishes.

My work is constantly evolving. Each collection represents a distinct mood, palette, and set of textures. Yet from season to season, the designs also show a remarkable consistency that's rare in an industry known for mercurial swings. Our customers always recognize Babette designs. At the same time, each season brings the thrill of anticipation and the delight of discovery.

I never could have reached this fortieth anniversary without the talents and dedication of an extraordinary group of people: loyal employees like Elfriede Griffey, who was the second person I hired and who still works with us; my brilliant co-designer Josephine Tchang, with whom I enjoy a true meeting of the minds; Leung Tang, our creative master pleater; Debbie Harder, our director of sales, who has helped us open new Babette stores and reach new markets; and my husband and business partner Steven Pinsky, who combines vision and realism in equal measure. Heartfelt thanks to all of you—and to the rest of our wonderful Babette team.

And I thank you, our customers, for discovering us, returning to us, and telling your friends about us. You inspire me!

Babette

Foreword

I discovered Babette nearly twenty years ago, when I bought my first Babette coat. It was reversible (blue on one side, gray on the other) and I remember thinking: *This piece of clothing is clever. It's unusual. It's intellectually interesting.*

And I looked terrific when I wore it.

Since then I've integrated many Babette garments into my wardrobe, and I've come to know Babette herself as a friend and fellow artist. I've always admired Babette's independence; she doesn't copy, and she doesn't yield to fashion fads. As a public artist myself, I know how hard it is to maintain a distinctive and inventive vision in the art world. To do it in the fashion world, and to succeed commercially as well as aesthetically, is rare indeed.

But here's the secret of Babette's clothes: they aren't merely "art to wear." They are democratic in the best possible sense—in their merging of form and function, they respect women of all ages, shapes, and lifestyles. They always look only like Babette and also, paradoxically, only like the woman who wears them.

Fashion is often said to be about change—what's in and what's out. With Babette, though, fashion is a stimulating conversation that you, the customer, have with the designer and her ideas. And like other loyal Babette fans, I'm always eager for the next conversation to commence.

Topher Delaney, San Francisco

Imaginative.

My clothes—designed with simple strong lines and colors—are intended for the woman who's not too caught up in the current fashion thing, but who still wants to look contemporary and sensational.

– Babette, quoted in the Cleveland Plain Dealer, *1975*

There were two approaches to design in the late 1960s: the tie-dye, decorative, hippie-style approach and the clean, minimalist Scandinavian aesthetic. I was influenced by the second approach, and by the purity of modern architecture. I always believed that function dictates form: the guiding principle of the Bauhaus design movement. And I was always inspired by beautiful fabric. Then as now, I would begin each season's collection by looking at fabric and deciding what stories I wanted to tell with it. Color and texture allowed me to shape a narrative.

– *Babette*

Left: Babette (in back) models a wool jersey dress from an early collection.

Opposite: Three advertising photographs taken in 1972.

Previous spread: Caftan silhouettes in cotton-polyester blend, from a mid–1970s collection.

  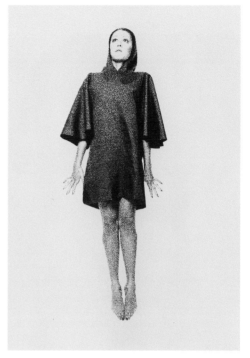

I always knew I'd be a designer and that I'd have
my own business—there was simply no question about it.
And I always knew I'd design clothes that every woman
could wear, regardless of age, size, or shape.

– Babette

Dramatic.

Coats are complicated. The pattern is a challenge; the shape is a challenge. The lining, the pockets, the collar, the fastenings. But it's all worth it, because a coat is a special garment. It makes an entrance and an impression—the first impression the world gets of you.

– Babette

Dramatic silhouettes from
a mid–1980s collection.

The original pleated raincoat
in pleated polyurethane, from
a mid–1980s collection.

Opposite: Pleated coat in
polyurethane-coated rayon
with a metallic finish,
mid–1980s.

I read in *Women's Wear Daily* that the designer Mary McFadden was going to launch a raincoat line. She was famous for pleats, so I assumed her raincoats would be pleated. I decided to beat her to it. I had 500 yards of polyurethane fabric in my studio, and I had it all pleated and made into raincoats. McFadden's raincoats? Not pleated, after all. Mine were the first.

– Babette

Pleated.

The process of creating Babette clothing is very much like the process of movie making. Babette is the director, but it takes an entire team to execute her concepts. It's a single vision with many hands.

– Steven Pinsky

Master pleater Leung Tang, co-designer Josephine Tchang, and Babette with a pattern pleat-in-progress.

A single pleated garment may be touched by as many as twelve workers during its creation.

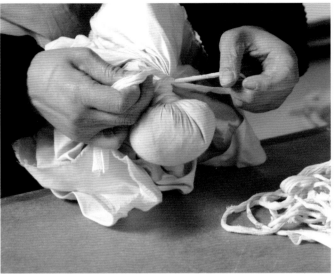

Above: Bolts of fabric await cutting in the Oakland design studio. The fabric—most of it manufactured in Japan—was ordered six months previously at Première Vision, the fabric exposition held twice yearly in Paris. *Top right:* Two workers create "paper-bag" pleats by crumpling microfiber fabric between their fingers, then gathering it into a tight ball and encasing it in a fabric sleeve. The intense heat of an industrial autoclave "pressure cooks" the pleats. *Bottom right:* To create pattern pleats, fabric is sandwiched between hand-scored sheets of beaming paper, then weighted with wooden blocks, tightly compressed, and heat-set.

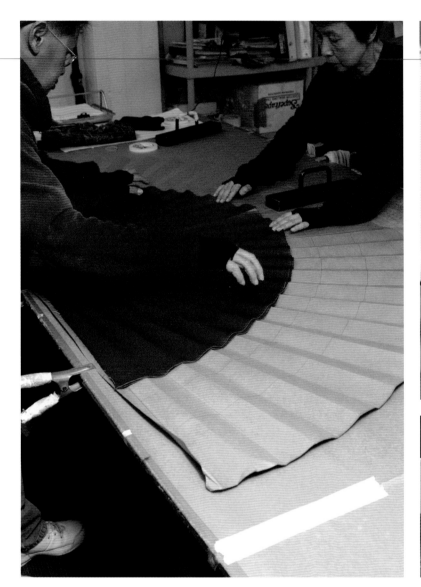

Above: Pattern pleating using fan-shaped beaming paper. Pattern pleating is an ancient art; hieroglyphics in Egyptian tombs depict pattern-pleating tools virtually identical to those used today. *Top right:* Pattern pieces being cut. *Bottom right:* Blouse fronts and sleeves emerge from the pleating machine.

The Babette team, circa 1980. *Left to right:* Dian Bloomquist, Luli Emmons, Elfriede Griffey, Angela Hernandez, Babette, Ilona Kraynick.

Early examples of pleated sportswear, from 1992 and 1993 collections. *Far left:* Double-layer chiffon dress in combination pleats. *Left:* blouse in combination box pleat; chevron skirt from a pattern discovered in a Los Angeles pleating factory.

Opposite: Cap-sleeve flower-pleat blouse, Summer 2007. The blouse is pleated twice, first by hand and then in a paper pattern.

A 2002 collection of form-fitting, cube-pleated separates in iridescent microfiber.

Textured.

I'm drawn to textures that tell a story: the sleekness of polyurethane, the inviting softness of boiled wool, the shape shifting of memory fabric.

— *Babette*

Wool embroidery
adds dimension to a
pleated polyester coat
from 2004.

Opposite:
Left: Jacket, Fall 2007.
Right: Pleated skirt, with
Mona Lisa transfer print,
circa 1999.

Previous spread:
Crisp cotton (*left*)
and double-weave linen
(*right*) shirt-jackets, both
from 1997-1998.

Contrast piping on the
portrait collar and ruffled
hem emphasize the design
of this fluid silk dress
from a 1980 collection.

Opposite: From 1980,
a line of soft wool-jersey
dresses. The dress in the
center is the popular
"butterfly" silhouette,
which slipped over the
head without fasteners.

Effortless.

When I work with Babette, I have no limitations. I can play with the best fabrics, use the best trims, let my imagination roam. I can create anything that fits our image. It's a designer's dream to have that freedom.

– Josephine Tchang

My clothes make a
major statement while
being completely
comfortable, versatile,
and easy to wear.

– *Babette*

Two iridescent textures: smooth and scrunchy.

Opposite: "Paper doll" separates, from the Summer 2003 collection, were designed to be scissor-altered by the customer. The mini-cube pleat was as stretchy and forgiving as a knit.

45

Timeline

Encouraged by her mother, a glove designer, 13-year-old Babette Wiener enrolls in a patternmaking class at Meyer School of Design in New York City.

——

As a new Fashion Institute of Technology graduate, Babette travels to Denmark in 1962 through an exchange program sponsored by the Scandinavian-American Foundation. Her assignment: designing raincoats. It is her first professional experience with raincoats—but not her last.

——

Resettled in San Francisco in 1964, Babette becomes the sole designer for Malco Modes, which makes rain-coats, car coats, and, unpredictably, square-dance dresses. Square-dance fashion is known for being conservative and formulaic; Babette causes a stir by shortening skirts. Customers love the change.

——

The Babette label debuts in April 1968 with ten styles including dresses, coats, capes, and caftans in strong, dramatic silhouettes influenced by design icons Bonnie Cashin and Rudi Gernreich. The fabric is a cotton-polyester blend; each garment is available in five or six colors. The collection is featured in home-design stores, including a new shop that Babette and her husband open in Sausalito: McDermott's.

From the start, Babette does all the designing. Her first employee is a seamstress. The second person she hires is also a seamstress: Elfriede Griffey, who is still with the company nearly forty years later.

——

The art-to-wear crafts—weaving, dyeing, fabric painting—flourish in the 1970s. Babette does freelance design work for a group of textile artisans, and teaches "No More Ponchos" at a craft school in Maine.

——

The original Babette raincoats, made of pleated polyurethane, are introduced in the early 1980s. Babette devises the technique and finds a Bay Area company to do the pleating.

——

During a sales call in the late 1980s, a salesman shows Babette samples of a revolutionary new fabric called microfiber—tightly woven polyester that breathes and handles beautifully. Recognizing its potential, Babette beings designing the first pleated microfiber separates. Even after pleating, the fabric remains pleasurably soft.

——

The first Babette retail store opens in San Francisco, on South Park Street, in 1991. It also serves as a design studio and outlet store. It closes in 2003, when the new Sutter Street store opens.

Steven Pinsky joins the company in 1991, overseeing production and sales.

——

When a Bay Area pleating contractor decides to close his operation in 1995, Babette Inc. buys the company—including the pleating equipment, which remains in the existing plant. Two years later, Babette Inc. takes over the entire 20,000-square-foot facility. Babette remains a rarity among U.S. garment manufacturers, most of whom contract all production to overseas facilities.

——

Babette eau de cologne spray is introduced in 2005. A crisp, elegant blend, it combines citrus top notes with mid-notes of dry sage, lavender, lily, and rose and an amber and jasmine dry-out. Each bottle is dressed in a signature red pleated sleeve.

——

Working with outside technical designers Babette begins including sweaters and other knitwear to the line in 2001. Three years later, she embarks on a collaboration with Texas knit designer Joel Childress; in 2008 Babette acquires the Childress label, which allows for expansion of Babette knitwear.

——

Babette Inc. celebrates its fortieth anniversary in 2008. ■

Credits

PHOTOGRAPHY

Page 1: Larry Keenan

Page 4: John Storey, *San Francisco Chronicle*

Pages 6/7: Michelle McCarron

Page 8: Larry Keenan

Page 11: Larry Keenan

Pages 12/13: Larry Keenan

Pages 14/15: Larry Keenan

Page 16: Paul Cruz

Pages 18/19: Paul Cruz

Pages 20/21: David Perez

Page 22: Larry Keenan

Pages 24/25: Steven Pinsky

Page 26: Steven Pinsky

Page 27: Albert Morse

Page 28: Photographer unknown

Page 29: Steven Pinsky

Pages 30/31: Larry Keenan

Page 32: Michelle McCarron

Pages 34/35: David Perez

Page 36: Steven Pinsky

Page 37: Michelle McCarron (*left*), Steven Pinsky

Page 38: John Ladislaw

Page 39: Paul Cruz

Page 40: Larry Keenan

Pages 42/43: Larry Keenan

Page 44: Larry Keenan

Page 45: David Perez

Page 46: David Perez

ACKNOWLEDGMENTS

Our thanks to Ryan del Norté, the designer who took several boxes of photographs and turned them into a beautiful, coherent chronicle.

To writer Nancy Friedman, who researched the story behind the images and created a narrative to complement them.

And to proofreader Carolyn Ricketts, who gave the manuscript its final polish.

Finally, sincere thanks to the gifted photographers with whom we've worked over the last four decades and whose vision has reflected, enhanced, and advanced our own.

BABETTE FLAGSHIP STORES

NEW YORK - SoHo
137 Greene Street, New York, NY 10012

CHICAGO - Downtown
25 East Huron Street, Chicago, IL 60611

SAN FRANCISCO - Union Square
361 Sutter Street, San Francisco, CA 94108

PORTLAND - Pearl District
208 NW 13th Avenue, Portland, OR 97209

SCOTTSDALE - Downtown
7051 E. Fifth Avenue, Scottsdale, AZ 85251

WWW.BABETTESF.COM